WHAT YOU NEVER KNEW ABOUT

OLIVIA

RODRIGO

by Dr. Nafeesah Allen

CAPSTONE PRESS
a capstone imprint

This is an unauthorized biography.

Spark is published by Capstone Press, an imprint of Capstone
1710 Roe Crest Drive, North Mankato, Minnesota 56003
capstonepub.com

Copyright © 2024 by Capstone. All rights reserved. No part of this publication may be reproduced in whole or in part, or stored in a retrieval system, or transmitted in any form or by any means, electronic, mechanical, photocopying, recording, or otherwise, without written permission of the publisher.

Library of Congress Cataloging-in-Publication Data
Names: Allen, Nafeesah, author.
Title: What you never knew about Olivia Rodrigo / Nafeesah Allen.
Description: North Mankato, Minnesota : Capstone Press, 2023. | Series: Behind the scenes biographies | Includes bibliographical references and index. | Audience: Ages 9 to 11 | Audience: Grades 4-6 | Summary: "Olivia Rodrigo was already a successful actress when she jumped onto the music scene. Her album, *Sour,* climbed the charts with songs such as "Drivers License" and "Good 4 U." But what does she do when she's not acting and dancing? High-interest details and bold photos will draw in reluctant and struggling readers, while carefully leveled text will leave them feeling confident"— Provided by publisher.
Identifiers: LCCN 2022058782 (print) | LCCN 2022058783 (ebook) | ISBN 9781669049463 (hardcover) | ISBN 9781669049500 (paperback) | ISBN 9781669049517 (pdf) | ISBN 9781669049531 (kindle edition) | ISBN 9781669049548 (epub)
Subjects: LCSH: Rodrigo, Olivia—Juvenile literature. | Singers—United States—Biography—Juvenile literature. | Actors—United States—Biography—Juvenile literature. | LCGFT: Biographies.
Classification: LCC ML3930.R634 A55 2022 (print) | LCC ML3930.R634 (ebook) | DDC 782.42164092 [B]—dc23/eng/20221206
LC record available at https://lccn.loc.gov/2022058782
LC ebook record available at https://lccn.loc.gov/2022058783

Editorial Credits
Editor: Mandy Robbins; Designer: Heidi Thompson; Media Researcher: Jo Miller; Production Specialist: Tori Abraham

Image Credits
Alamy: White House Photo, 27, INSTAR Images LLC, 21; Getty Images: Cindy Ord, 13, Jamie McCarthy, 19, Jenny Anderson, 8, Jon Kopaloff, 7, Joseph Okpako, 15, 25, Kevin Mazur, 18, Matt Winkelmeyer, 29, Rich Fury, 10, Rodin Eckenroth, 9; Newscom: WavyPeter / SplashNews, 17; Shutterstock: Alexandru Nika, 11 (bottom), Byjeng, 12, 13 (gems), Dimitra Merziemekidou, 5, Fred Duval, 22, Frogella, 12 (hand, flower, rainbow), Kathy Hutchins, Cover, Liliana Danila, 12 (butterflies), linear_design, 24, selisegator, 28, SP-Photo, 11 (top), studiovin, 16-17, tanuha2001, 23 (right), Tarzhanova, 12, 13 (glitter stars), Tigerline, 20, Tinseltown, 4, TK 1980, 26, Ziyafet Haciyeva, 23 (left)

All internet sites appearing in back matter were available and accurate when this book was sent to press.

TABLE OF CONTENTS

All-American Girl 4

Pop Quiz! 6

True Passion 8

License to Drive 10

Family Matters 14

Fashion Focus 16

Hanging with Olivia 18

Social Media Stats 22

Close Causes 24

Sour Prom 28

Glossary 30

Read More 31

Internet Sites 31

Index 32

About the Author 32

Words in **bold** are in the glossary.

ALL-AMERICAN
GIRL

Olivia Rodrigo has been a Disney star. She shot to musical fame with her song "Drivers License." But you knew that. What don't you know? Time to find out!

What would Olivia save in a fire? Her American Girl dolls! She starred in *Grace Stirs Up Success*, an American Girl movie.

POP QUIZ!

Are you a true fan? Fill in the blanks:

1. Where did Olivia write most of her songs?

2. What McDonald's breakfast is her favorite?

3. What was her first on-screen appearance?

4. Her childhood pet was a ____ named Stripes.

FACT

Olivia's fans call themselves,
Rodrigans, Rodriganators, Livies,
Olivinators, and even DMV clerks.

1. in her bedroom **2.** oatmeal

3. an Old Navy commercial **4.** snake

7

TRUE
PASSION

Olivia loves songwriting. She wrote "All I Want" for *High School Musical: The Musical.*

Olivia looks up to female singer/songwriters. Some old-school **idols** are Alanis Morissette and Gwen Stefani. She's also a fan of Lorde, Billie Eilish, and Cardi B. Country singer Kacey Musgraves even makes her list.

Cardi B.

LICENSE TO
DRIVE

When Olivia released "Drivers License," it topped the iTunes chart in hours. The song broke Spotify's **record** for the most streams in one day (for a non-holiday song). It topped out at 17 million on January 12, 2021.

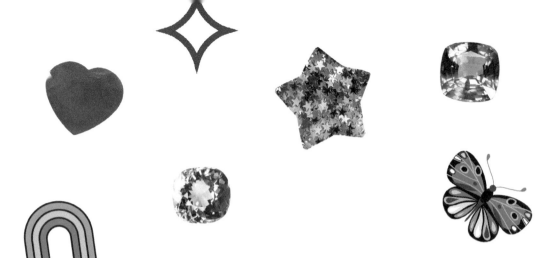

"Drivers License" was number one in the U.S. for eight weeks. The song also went to number one in Australia, the U.K., New Zealand, and Norway.

Olivia's full album, *Sour*, dropped on May 21, 2021. It made a splash on Spotify! Its songs were played over 385 million times in seven days.

13

FAMILY MATTERS

Olivia is tight with her parents. Her father is Filipino-American. Olivia loves her family's Filipino traditions. A favorite is making special egg rolls called "lumpias."

Her mom is the first person she plays her new songs for. She's also the person who pushed O to take piano lessons. Olivia didn't always like them. It's safe to say they've paid off!

FASHION
FOCUS

When it comes to fashion, Olivia doesn't buy new. She would rather **thrift** or swap clothes with friends. Olivia disagrees with how the fashion **industry** works. Many workers aren't paid enough. Lots of old clothes end up in the trash too.

HANGING WITH
OLIVIA

Olivia and Iris Apatow

Olivia has a fun group of friends. Close pals include Conan Gray, Lydia Night, Iris Apatow, and Madison Hu.

Ethan Wacker makes the list too. Wait! Didn't they date? Yep, but they've stayed friends. They often comment on each other's Instagram posts.

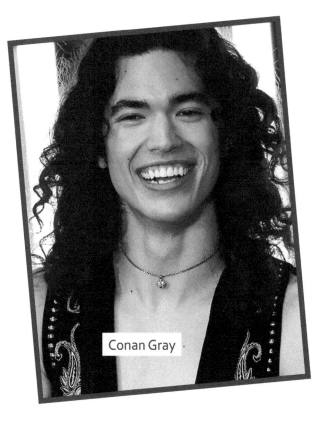

Conan Gray

How far would Olivia go for her pals? She is willing to Facetime her friends with a fake emergency if they are on a bad date. A friend did it for her once. They faked that they were being robbed!

FACT

Olivia's "*Sour* Tour Prom Night" included her core friends Conan Gray, Lydia Night, Iris Apatow, and Madison Hu.

SOCIAL MEDIA
STATS

Olivia uses Twitter and Instagram to talk about her work and important issues. She has almost 2 million Twitter followers. On Insta, about 30 million people follow her!

Want to see Olivia's silly side? Check out her TikToks. She has more than 15 million followers there.

CLOSE
CAUSES

Olivia stands up for what she believes in. She is all about equality and **diversity**. She supports LGBTQ causes and Black Lives Matter. She has also been a speaker for the Geena Davis Institute on Gender in the Media.

Olivia also promotes girls in science! She's part of the "She Can STEM" **campaign**.

Speaking of science, President Joe Biden asked Olivia to encourage people to get **COVID-19** shots. She made social media videos with the President and Dr. Anthony Fauci.

SOUR PROM

Olivia's album, *Sour*, was a huge hit. She turned that success into a 27-minute live video performance. She crowned two prom queens and brought them onstage.

Olivia even surprised eight lucky fans. They got to be her "dates" to the *Sour Prom* video premiere.

FACT

In 2022, Olivia won the Grammy for The Best Pop Vocal Album for *Sour*.

Glossary

campaign (kam-PAYN)—an organized effort

COVID-19 (KO-vid nine-TEEN)—a mild to severe respiratory illness that is caused by a coronavirus

diversity (dye-VUR-si-tee)—the inclusion of people of different ethnicities, genders, abilities, sexual orientation, belief systems, and other types of differences.

idol (EYE-duhl)—a person greatly admired or looked up to

industry (IN-duh-stree)—a business sector that produces a product or provides a service

record (REK-urd)—when something is done better than anyone has ever done it before

thrift (THRIFT)—to buy at second-hand shops or garage sales

Read More

Marx, Mandy R. *What You Never Knew About Taylor Swift*. North Mankato, MN: Capstone Press, 2022.

Rose, Rachel. *Olivia Rodrigo: Actor and Singer.* Minneapolis: Bearport Publishing Company, 2023.

Schwartz, Heather E. *Olivia Rodrigo: Hit Singer-Songwriter*. Minneapolis: Lerner Publications, 2023.

Internet Sites

High School Musical: The Musical: The Series
disneyplus.com/series/high-school-musical-the-musical-the-series/22p0ndod96BX

Olivia Rodrigo: Home
oliviarodrigo.com

Olivia Rodrigo: Instagram
instagram.com/oliviarodrigo/?hl=en

Index

American Girl, 5

Biden, President Joe, 26
Black Lives Matter, 24

childhood pet, 6, 7
COVID-19, 26

Disney, 5

fashion, 16
Fauci, Dr. Anthony, 26
friends, 16, 18, 19, 20

Geena Davis Institute on
  Gender in the Media, 24

*High School Musical: The
  Musical*, 9

Instagram, 19, 23
iTunes, 11

LGBTQ causes, 24

McDonald's, 6, 7

Olivia's songs, 6, 14
  "All I Want," 9
  "Drivers License," 5, 11, 12

parents, 14
piano lessons, 14

"She Can STEM" campaign, 26
Sour, 12, 20, 28, 29
Spotify, 11, 12

TikTok, 23
Twitter, 23

About the Author

Dr. Nafeesah Allen is a world traveler, wife, and mom. Her family speaks English, Spanish, and Portuguese, and loves good music. Her favorite activity is to host surprise dance parties in her kitchen.